Alice,

Don't worry...

Will Crane

How I Arrived Here

How I Arrived Here

A Memoir

Ani Crane

Soul Attitude Press

Soul Attitude Press
P.O. Box 1656
Pinellas Park, FL 33780

FIRST EDITION

ISBN 978-1-939181-44-2

To my Ancestors,
my Children,
my Grandchildren,
my Great Grandchildren
and Romeo
with love

Table of Contents

Preface

In reviewing my life, healing what needed to be healed, forgiving what needed to be forgiven including myself in order to move forward with as clean a slate as possible, it came to my attention that my children did not know the piece that came before them: my romance - how I met and fell in love with their father. I felt they needed to know this. So I set about writing it for them. With this piece set down I was inspired to chronicle the rest of my journey- how I arrived at the place of piece, joy and love where I now reside... in Florida. I'm free, I'm happy and I'm greatly loved.

Introduction

'To Life Le Chaim'

I love my life! My life is beautiful! It keeps getting better and better. Every day is another day in paradise. It sounds corny but it's true. My life has all the ingredients to make it so: beauty, health, awareness, order, fulfillment, creative expression, ease, love, rewarding relationships, abundance and prosperity ... the intangibles that make life worth living and that money can't buy.

I chose a spiritual path to unravel the tangle of challenges that I faced in mid life. I sought enlightenment, that natural, effortless state. I sought a healthy body through yoga, tai chi, swimming and a healthy delicious food plan and education ... only to find out later there's nothing to do and nowhere to go, just do the next right thing that arises in the present and take an inspired action. I'm still mastering this because you never get it wrong and you never get it done. I am happily incomplete. Here is my story of how I arrived here in this time, space reality.

Part I

My romance story
Memories warm my sweet heart
Bringing me back there

I.

My Romance

'Just One Look'

Me- Catholic school girl complete with uniform & saddle shoes. Him- high school dropout with leather jacket, dungarees & cigarettes. All the ingredients needed for true romance.

He & his best friend Tommy Brennan hanging out @ the local candy store were a couple of cool guys... they were also sweet. Me & my friends thought we were cool too... for Catholic school girls, after all we did get away with smoking in the boiler room of our beloved 'Wisdom'. And there was the match... it ignited spontaneously. I was 16, he was 18.

Setting: local Candy Store hang out...I walked by many times on my way to call for my friend, the guys offered friendly greetings. Best friend Tommy Brennan had a Humber Hawk, a rare foreign car in those days. and the guys took great pride in keeping it shiny.

Next scene: @ the beach. Every summer weekend the neighborhood kids would hop on the bus & head to Rockaway-116 St was the hot spot. Me & my bestie Rae Acquavella made the scene every Sunday. We thought we were 'the cat's meow '& delighted in our new swim suits. On one Sunday when family visitors required me to stay @ home, 'He' asked my friend Rae 'Where is She?' interest mounts. On another occasion, a sweetly amusing one, was when all the gang went out on the sandbar to play. As time passed, the tide came in & it was necessary to swim back to shore. As I reached the shore I looked down & there He was still swimming for dear life not as comfortable in the water as I. So sweet! It was shortly after that we began dating in earnest.

Dating in the 50's: One of our favorite dates was a Sunday afternoon matinee @ the Casino movie which was followed by a light supper of bacon,lettuce & tomato sandwiches on toast compliments of his Mom. (to this day still a favorite of mine)

I also had baby sitting jobs & He was allowed to keep me company after I put the kids to bed...which led to heavy petting. And the raging hormones of youth raged on.

There were many more beach days & nights too, we would stroll along the boardwalk happy & in love making plans for the future.I was completing my high school degree & He was going to school at night to study Diesel engines.

Engagement-happy days! Right after my graduation we got engaged & planned to marry the following Sept. That period of time in our relationship was idyllic. We were young & in love. It was the 50's & life was innocent & simple. We went on double dates to the drive in with my school pal & her beau.I remember one Easter Sunday dressed in our spring finery we drove into Manhattan with Tommy & his girlfriend in the famous Humber Hawk or was it a Mercury coupe then? Anyway Gatsby had nothing on us!I proudly wore my picture hat, the one & only time I ever donned such a chapeau. It was a magical time! And I'll never forget the Christmas He gave me a Benrus Embraceable watch. He smelled like ivory soap & dentyne gum. I was swept away. I was so swept away that my virginity was swept away as well. Unsophisticated as I was that joy led to our love child, beautiful daughter Joanne.

Love & Marriage & a baby carriage: The wedding date was moved up & we happily moved into our first home, a cute apartment in Middle Village to await the arrival of our new baby. I was 18, He was 20. We were both happy & excited over our new family. Both of us were working in Manhattan @ that time so we decided to take a Red Cross course after work 'How to care for a new baby'. This proved very helpful for it gave us both confidence when handling our new doll baby.

The Hanover Bank Social Circle: My first job out of H.S. was @ Hanover Bank. Myself along with a half a dozen other Catholic school graduates began our 'banking career'. There was Yvonne, Kathy, Lori, Lucy & Lillian as I recall. We gals got along so well & since all of us were dating it turned into a fun social group as well. We had many house parties over the years and to this day I am still in constant contact with my BFF Yvonne (we both live in Gulfport, FL) These memories & friendships are precious to me now.

Our growing family: Being an only child, I wanted a sibling for Joanne...and 14 months later along came Glenn firstborn son. We had the perfect family, a girl & a boy.

To our surprise & joy, one year later we were blessed with a set of identical twins: Ken & Chris arrived in perfect health. By now we were living in the projects in Far Rockaway (we always had a warm spot in our hearts for the beach).We were the proud parents of 4, our family had doubled. (I think it was at Rae & Phil's wedding, we got swept away...again & 9 months later...)

The Projects: Friends & Neighbors: Living in the projects had some benefits: nursery school @ age 3 for the kids ... some welcome relief for this young mother of 4.

At this point in the story my Catholic school teaching played havoc...birth control is a sin. And so nature took it's course & #5 Gregg Steven, a robust baby boy was born. I was 22, He was 24, we had our work cut out for us and we rose to the occasion as best we could. My next door neighbor Greta met my needs in many ways: friendship, tea & sympathy, playdates w/ the kids and an occasional double date at the movies with Greta & her husband, a special treat for us. Greta & I took a modern dance class @ the 5 Towns 'Y' which was a much needed outlet for us both, she had 3 small children & I had my tribe of 5. We enjoyed the class so much we both enrolled our daughters in a class for 3-4 year olds. When things got overwhelming as they often did, I could go next door, the kids would play & I would get some much needed tea & sympathy. I realize now what a blessing Greta was to me.

Payday Presents: Looking back I appreciate the great sacrifices involved in raising 5 kids and I have no regrets. I did it my way! I had to wash, dress & feed 6 every day, myself & the 5 babies.He had to work 3 jobs to support the gang. He made a ritual of bringing home little presents or treats for the kids on payday which would thrill & delight them. Things could get chaotic at home but I always had my little helpers in the projects. 2 pre-teen sisters were always anxious to help me & make a bit of spare change. They always seemed to show up at a crucial moment when I couldn't find one of the kids shoes & in no time Voila!

here it is (for a quarter-well worth it)

Walks & Talks & Beaches & Parks: Greta & I loved taking the kids outside when the weather was nice, it was worth all the effort to see their happy faces. Beach excursions took alot more effort but seeing the kids frolicking in the water made it all worthwhile. To this day my kids all enjoy the beach & water sports. And so do I!

The end of this era came when we were able to buy our own home in Richmond Hill, Queens... the home I had grown up in. And so a new chapter begins with the education of the 5 kids in Catholic School-always a good education.

He was the love of my life, a family man , a good provider & a devoted father.

Rest in peace J.K.

PS. The disease of Alcoholism played havoc in this beautiful story... we learn & we move forward & create healthier lives the next go round & appreciate the gifts.

I'm so proud of my kids all building strong families & raising wonderful kids.

Good genes! ;-)

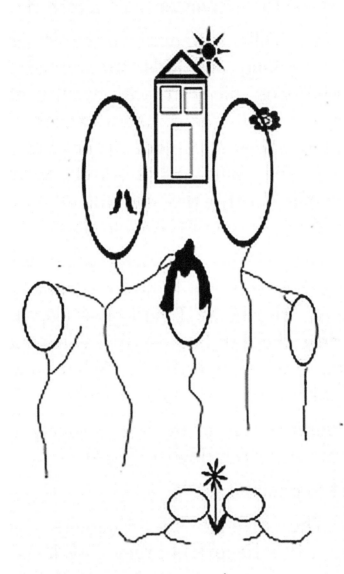

The wonder years' joy
A time of innocent bliss
A piece of my life

II.

The Wonder Years

'Our House'

And so it was that we moved into our house in Richmond Hill, Queens where we lived together for the next 15 years. I had grown up in that very house and my father before me; this would be the third generation. It was a time of education for all ,learning and growing in many different ways: the 5 kids were enrolled in Gate of Heaven Catholic School where I had attended grammar school. At that time he was working nights @ the post office @ Kennedy Airport and learning electrical engineering as an apprentice with my High School friend Gail's husband on the side and later taking classes. He was what you would call a self made man later entering the engineering field with no formal degree, quite remarkable actually. I was working as a paraprofessional in the local high school and going to Queens College for my teaching degree. It took me 10 years at night. It was a pretty busy time what with the kids hectic schedule of extra curricular activities such as brownies,cub scouts, fife & drum corps, play rehersals, soft ball, basketball, track & wrestling. Summertime was funtime @ Rockaway Beach several times a week & meeting up with friend Rae & her 4 kids; mom's could relax & catch up while kids had fun playing & swimming in the water & just being free. Whitney Pond Pool & picnics at Valley Stream State Park were also on the agenda. In the wintertime a trip to an ice skating rink or into NYC to Radio City Music Hall for holiday shows were a special treat.

Joanne took to school like a duck to water always making us proud...the boys-not so much with so much energy to spare. I would often hear the term hyper-active or short attention span from the teachers. That's where sports came in handy, a good outlet.

I can still remember the excitement when my children received their First Holy Communion and Confirmation, such a blessing. A celebration always followed with friends & family. The boys became altar boys who assist the priest at Mass...they looked so angelic up there on the altar.

As they grew older the boys wanted to earn more spending money and took on paper routes which Dad would often help out with on a Sunday when papers were 'fat' & heavy. Joanne used her brains for earning extra cash. We had several families on the block from Italy so as well as babysitting the kids she helped the Mamas learn English- a born teacher & mother. Her charges adored her and the mothers appreciated her help. They compensated her well & loved her dearly.

Once my husband left the post office and became an electrical engineer our prosperity increased and so did his alcohol consumption. We had a social life which was house parties, block parties & eating out with other couples, the typical activities of that era. We started taking family vacations and later on getaways for us as a couple. I recall a trip to the Hamptons & Shapanack Dude Ranch for the family and Paradise Island Club Med for us.Constant drinking was a source of discomfort to me and tension in the home. Alcoholic? I was in denial. One of the saddest events of that period was when Gregg the youngest then 5 was hit by a car. That Saturday started out fine,we had a plan to go get some seafood @ Sheepshead Bay with Rae & Phil. I was excited!Joe who was still working nights then came home & informed me he didn't want to go. Period...no discussion ...and off to bed he went. Not a happy camper I put plan B into action...send the 2 oldest to church to confession and take a walk on the avenue with the 3 youngest and visit a friend for tea & sympathy (again).While I was visiting the three boys were outside playing a dangerous game-daring each other to run into the street. As fate would have it Gregg got clipped and lay in the street unconscious. Chaos ensued, an ambulance was called and we were off to Jamaica Hospital. I called my mother to meet the kids returning home from church. My Mom was my Angel,always there for me in time of need- if one of the kids were sick & couldn't go to school,she would watch them for me when I went to work.Another difficult issue to cope with at that time was my husband's deep sleep habit. The police came to inform him of the accident and with no answer to the door bell they had to break into the house & the bedroom to rouse him with this awful news. It was not the Wonder Years of TV. The recovery period of Gregg took a week for him to regain consciousness & come out of the coma. The neurologist had told me on day one that he would recover completely. I clung with deep faith to that hope. Friends rallied round and brought food for the family as I was at the hospital every day. I would call every morning to see if there was any change. On the 7th day as I was waiting for the nurse I heard Gregg's voice asking for Gumby & Pokey his favorite toys. I cried with joy, I knew the siege was over. but this event was only a symptom of the trouble in paradise and there would be more to come.

The teen years were harrowing with the boys as things swirled more & more out of control...the major problems being drugs and absenteeism from school. It was not a day at the beach. As parents we could not agree on how to handle these problems. Me being all for education was to enforce attendance., he being the self made man said if they don't go to school take them out & let them work. I was heartbroken.

The drugs were another story: my view- a rehab situation; his view- kick him out of the house. This plan did not work to change anything. I was devastated! A week later back in the house which was robbed twice by the druggie circle of friends... same old, same old. This ship was sinking fast. With these ingredients the desired outcome of harmony was not happening.

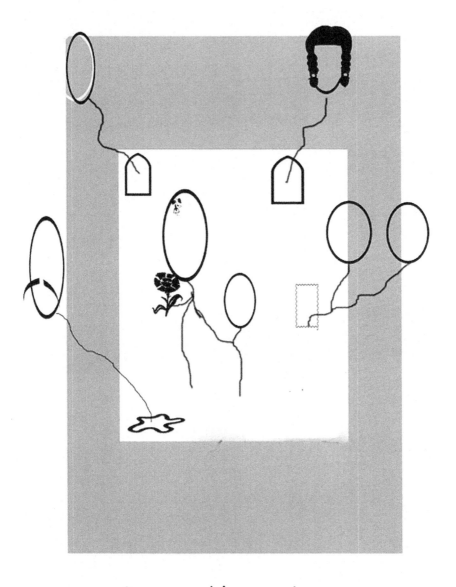

Some problems arise
Beginning of the ending
Overwhelming time

III.

Beginning of the End

'Hard Times Are Over'

In order to get some kind of plan in place or solution to all the overwhelming problems arising, I called for a family council meeting. I opened with: things have to change, we can't continue this way. My husband said, 'If you don't like it there's the door' And my oldest son seconded the motion... very Robert's rules of order. I never expected that outcome.

Within the month I got my belongings together & I took the door & they cursed me for it. I was 39, he was 41, Joanne was 20, Glenn was 19, the twins were 18 and Gregg was 17. Looking back now from the vantage point of maturity I realize I was wrong in that I did not consider the impact of my actions on my children. I was leaving my husband but they felt abandoned too.

Yes, breaking up is hard to do, the familiar vs. the unknown. But as the old saying goes, 'when one door closes, another opens.'

New beginnings: I took my clothes, my books, my music and some photos. It was the end of an era & the new beginning loomed ahead: scary/exciting I imagine for each family member. It had to be better than what had been.

I went directly to the ocean (Long Beach) to lick my wounds and heal & with the help of friends found my oasis @ the San Remo. Luckily I had my paraprofessional job in the High School and I was on the brink of getting my B.A. which would enable me to get a teaching position. I was connected. This piece did fall in to place with minimal angst. Good fortune smiled on me. Next item on the agenda: get a car.

Joanne was engaged @ this time and decided to forgo her college education and focus on her goal of marriage and having a family. The irony wasn't lost on me: her dream was beginning as mine was ending. Bittersweet. I was glad for her to have exciting plans to think about and carving her place in a new world of her own creation. She had one of the most beautiful weddings at a country club that I can remember and she made the most beautiful bride ever.

Her father and I attended and celebrated our daughter's marriage although our own hearts were broken. Her father paid the bill for the lovely affair, a good provider-true to form.

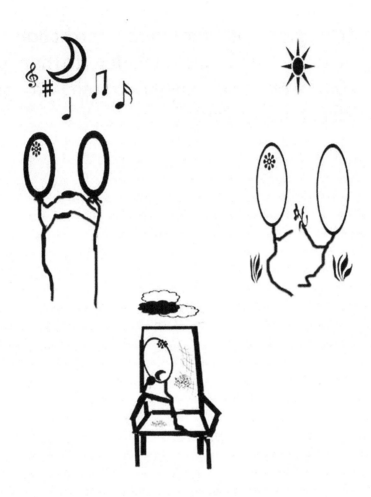

Exploration time
Dancing dating depression
A new and strange mix

IV.

Dancing Dating & Depression

'Last Dance'

I was in my 40's and single, not what I was planning. Most of my friends were couples. This was a big adjustment and a rude awakening to say the least. My married friends had plenty of advice for me on how to proceed... how would they know? They were safely married. I was the one 'out there' on the cutting edge... and it was scary yet exciting. When I finally got up the nerve to venture out to a singles dance event, I was fortunate to attract and meet a gentleman, TC who was honest and reliable if not too exciting but then I'd had all the excitement I could stand for awhile. He was just what the doctor ordered. This opportunity gave me company and attention (good for my self esteem) plus a date on Sat. nite; it also relieved me of having to get out there. TC also brought up comparisons with the ex who was my HS sweetheart & the father of my 5 children (and an alcoholic). This was depressing as there was no future there, no hope of a solution. To make matters worse, I started seeing my ex; he would come out to Long Beach and spend the weekend with me which was exciting yet painful when the weekend was over. What to do? Focus on building my new life and moving on. I set a few goals: get my masters degree and move into Manhattan. I had always dreamed of living there.

M.A.

B.A.

Theater Arts what fun
Getting a masters' degree
Playing my way there

V.

Completion : BA in Communication & Going for the Masters

'Pomp & Circumstance'

This was one of my roughest challenges yet. I had 6 months to go and would have my degree, a goal that took 10 years in coming. (but that's another story) I was living in Long Beach @ the time, newly separated from my husband of 21 years and 5 kids, emotionally raw. My internship or student teaching gig was at Seward Park H.S. in Manhattan/Chinatown and my classes in the evening were @ Queens College in Flushing. I got up @ 5am to drive from Long Island into Manhattan in time for class. Fun! After a long day of unruly, hormones raging H.S. students... I had time to spend prepping for the next day. Then I hopped in my car and drove to Queens College for 2 classes which demanded focus. Okay! And did I mention my $100 rust bucket car that I purchased from a friend was on the verge of a breakdown every day? In fact, this nightmare DID come true... a couple of times. Once in front of my door, thankfully, so I had to ask a favor for my ride into the city to meet my commitment. Another not so lucky time I broke down on the Manhattan Bridge. How this was resolved I'm still a blank. I do know I got to the job and a student of mine fixed the problem and I did drive home that evening. The coup de gras of nightmares: my car was towed away while parked in Manhattan and I had to humbly ask my ex who worked there for help. How humiliating was that? Ms. Independent... in a jam? Not a day at the beach. He did come and help me so I guess bearing him a brilliant daughter and 4 sons counted for something. Fond memories and exciting times. Bottom line, I did get my B.A. in Communication. I did get a teaching gig that I loved. I did help many students during my teaching career improve their reading, writing and speaking skills. Rewarding work! Je ne rien regrette! In loving memory of JK who helped me the day I most needed it.

One of the requirements of teaching for the NYC Board of Education was to get a master's degree within 5 years after starting your assignment. Now seemed like the time was right. Since I had to do it anyway, I decided to study an area I've always enjoyed and had fantasies of working in Theater Arts. this could only help with my teaching skills...give 'em the old razzle dazzle. I started out in NYU, a very prestigious school with high hopes. After one year I transferred to City College, a much more affordable establishment. The 3 years it took to complete the course at night and in the summertime (I was working days during the school year) were intense, yet exciting. I remember taking one summer semester @ Bklyn College and studying Japanese Kabuki Theater and Theater of Noh. I was very impressed and went w/ my classmates to see presentations @ Lincoln Center during the course.

In the midst of all this came the opportunity to move to Manhattan, my application to Independence Place (the deeper meaning of the name of the place is not lost on me) came up and off to Tribeca I went...but more about that later. For my theseis project I put on a production 'You Gotta Have Art'. I was involved in an art support group at that time and with the help of the members we wrote a show, directed it & preformed in it @ the Little Church Around the Corner. I invited my Professor/Mentor to attend. It was one of the most exciting, liberating times in my new life.

Loss grief sorrow pain
The final curtain falling
All over no more

VI.
Death & Divorce

'I'll Fly Away'

A divorce is kinda like a death of sorts. It's the end of life as you know it, being part of a couple- a husband or wife...the familiar. This change to single status brings up many emotions, some positive like relief and freedom but but many more negative ones such as failure, loss and self doubt. You go thru the 5 stages of grief; denial, anger, bargaining, sadness & finally acceptance. It is said that it takes one month for every year of marriage to heal. I was married 21 years and in 21 months I was not healed. Who said this anyway? Prove it! When one is going thru a divorce there are acting out signs in the behavior to ease the pain; drinking too much, wild sex and in my case- my driving suffered. I got more tickets in that time of my life than in my whole life...sliding thru stop signs was one of my offences. Couldn't stop, too painful, had to keep moving. It took a lot of effort on my part to correct that situation, but I did.

And then the day came approximately 2 years after the divorce of the big death in the family. JK died on Christmas day @ 48 years of age of liver failure. I was having Christmas dinner w/ my children when a call came in from their uncle who had heard from a neighbor of JK's in the east village; no answer to the knock on the door. Reminiscent of the time the police had to break in @ Gregg's accident, he slept like the dead but this time it was eternal sleep, there was to be no awakening. The twins drove into the city to meet their uncle and I stayed w/ Joanne & Gregg waiting to confirm the worst which we already knew but grimly awaited verification. It came & the end was here. The following week was a blur, arrangements were made & he was put to rest quickly as it was a holiday week so the funeral & burial had to be expedited. I contacted the Red Cross & they contacted Glenn & he flew home from his Air Force station in Germany. What was most poignant was that not a tear was shed by the children, they were shut down emotionally. After the burial his oldest sister hosted the repass for the family. I was not invited as we were divorced. My son Gregg & I went to a diner for a bite & comforted each other as best we could. And then it was home again to face life without one of the major players in the story. I returned to my home in Independence Plaza in Tribeca in a slump. The doorman had always been friendly to me. On impulse I invited him to come up for tea & sympathy after his shift was over explaining what I had just experienced. He did @ we had some tea & I appreciated the comfort of his company at that fork in the road of my life journey. I'm grateful that whenever there is a need, an angel has appeared.

Exit

Where is salvation?
Solution is the 12 steps
Yes! Halleluia

VII.

Tribeca, 12 Steps and Salvation!

'Amazing Grace'

Yes! I did it! I moved into Manhattan. I achieved my goal! Tribeca no less! On the Hudson River no less! View of the Statue of Liberty from the 33rd floor apartment no less! What a feeling! I started out in a town house & now I'm on the 33rd floor facing the Statue of Liberty! The implication is not lost on me. Rising up in the world.

Success is sweet! Nestled in my new home with a river view, I was flying high on this accomplishment. I thanked my lucky stars everyday. This was no time to sit back on my laurels. You got here ... what's next I asked myself? I'm on a roll. There were a few emotional issues that needed my attention. After all the years of living with an alcoholic, it never dawned on me ... go to AlAnon ... get yourself some help. Now seemed to be the perfect time to do that ... I could focus on myself and clear up some of the residue baggage from living in that system for so many years. So I went to my first AlAnon meeting @ Trinity Church downtown. This was to become a major support and new circle of friends for me...my tribe. How I blossomed & learned to take care of myself under this tutorledge. I was born again and I loved it. This group, these people turned into my family of choice, celebrating the holidays together, sober house parties and 4th of July fireworks ... learning to enjoy life again ... Fantastic! From AlAnon I was exposed to other 12 step meetings: D.A. for money issues, O.A. for food issues, and CoDA, later, for relationship issues. Instead of looking @ the alcoholic and wishing him to change and make me happy, I was looking @ myself and my issues and learning to make myself happy. What a wonderful realization! Like I woke up after all these years. What a wonderful world to discover!

Student ready k
Teacher appears miracle
Learning and teaching

VIII.

Teaching and Learning

'Forever Young'

I have had many joyful and satisfying moments during my teaching career as well as some challenging ones. But I was lucky, I worked with foreign students learning English who were so willing to learn and appreciative of the knowledge handed down to them. I worked with students from China, Japan, Korea & Russia among others. We bonded and became family. At every terms' end I would invite my students to my home for a pot luck of specialty dishes from their country. It was wonderful! One outstanding highlight of my teaching career was the term I introduced a pen pal project. I was teaching at NYU and BMCC at that time. I introduced these two groups of students to each other & had them write letters to their pen pal. As the relationships & skills built, I filmed each group introducing themselves to each other individually. This project met the needs of both groups in many ways: the NYU students wanted the opportunity to to relate to 'real Americans'. The BMCC students felt proud that they could 'help' these foreign students. The grand finale came when I invited NYU to visit BMCC, they brought show & tell items from their country. The BMCC group, being the hosts, baked cakes to welcome their new pen pals. Just remembering it makes my heart swell with pride. It was a big success. The project also worked to demystify the 'other', someone unlike themselves, realizing we all have the same wants and needs. I learned we all want to feel good about who we are and where we're from. This all played out beautifully in my classroom when given that opportunity. What a feeling! Aliveness, forever young!

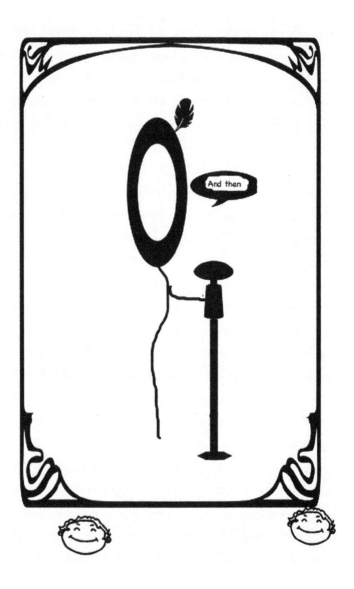

Travel, performing
Part of my autonomy
Exploring in out

IX.

Ani's Adventures in Autonomy

'Freebird'

After the big break up, I decided to channel my energy into creativity. A friend of mine was doing stand up comedy at open mike nights around town. Inspired, I wrote my material, 'Breaking Up is Hard To Do'. I couldn't feel sad and focus on writing at the same time so this exercise gave me some relief from the pain. Equipped with my material, off I went to the Eagle Tavern on 14th St downtown Manhattan. To my surprise, I recognized the Master of Ceremonies right away ... he had been working in the kitchen at an ashram I had attended in upstate New York. WOW! From ashram to comedy club! Anyway, this was a good sign I thought to myself to calm my nerves. You know what they say about stand up ... either you 'kill 'em' or 'you die'. Quite ominous! Going on first (getting it over with) helped relieve my nerves, so I got there extra early to sign up. And I was glad I had, half of the comics were waxing poetic on the same topic of breaking up, a popular one. Luckily I did not know this as I went first. Week after week I showed up, refining my material over and over again. I even invited friends to come and support me. What was I thinking? I really don't know how it went ... there was applause, that was good. All I do know it was a big step in healing from the break up. Next attempt: a one woman show 'Ani's Adventures in Autonomy' at an off off Bway space in Tribeca. To be continued ....

See the world woman
Discover countries cultures
Don't forget nature

IX. A.

Ani's Adventures Traveling

'Far Away Places'

Since my B.A. was complete & my divorce settlement was complete (sale of the family homestead) I decided give myself a graduation present: a trip. Where shall a newly divorced, newly graduated 40 year old woman go? After some deliberation I decided to go to Club Med in Guadelupe.

Excitement enough for this novice. On the plane there I met a girl from Brooklyn who was headed to the same place. We became fast friends and roommates. We delighted in all the water sports and single people in one place. This was the perfect playground for us.

Looking back the funniest thing that happened (it wasn't funny to me @ the time) was when we were bravely trying out the nude beach and my friend offered me her float. I joyously jumped freely in the water and leisurely floated away ... literally. I had floated out beyond my comfort zone and over toward the next beach which was not clothing optional. When given the choice to paddle back to the nude beach or the safety of the shore ... I chose the shore...to my embarrassment. I had to walk back to my beach in the buff with only the protection of the float. Woe is me! I'll never do that again. Yet in the retelling of it, it amused many a friend. Otherwise it was the perfect vacation for this gal to unwind from all the stress & challenges now behind me. The next chapter was bound to be an improvement.

Another fantastic vacation I remember was a barefoot cruise I took to the Caribbean; St. Marteen, St, Bart's, St. Kitts included. Being a Pisces my love of everything H2O this was ideal for me. I was living in Va. Bch at that time, my teaching career behind me and heavily into the esoteric, metaphysical and volunteering & studying at the ARE. The relaxed informal atmosphere of the barefoot cruise was just what I needed. It was quite exciting to be able to sleep outside on the deck under the stars. One of the fun times of this trip was the costume party they threw for us. I decided to go as a 'John' and enlisted two of my new friends to be my 'worker bees'.I wore a gold chain & undershirt, my 'Guido' look and won second prize losing first place place to a guy who made the loveliest ballerina. My prize was a bottle of champagne, that worked for me. All in good fun. I actually enjoyed being in character and 'bossing the girls' around.Oh & did I mention we barely averted a hurricane which added to the excitement. St. Marteen was French and Dutch, so the two sides of the island were a totally different flavor. Now St. Bart's, that was to my liking, more cosmopolitan. Exposure to all of these islands was an education in itself. Now I prefer a different type of travel: beauty, nature, culture and serenity are what I look for now.

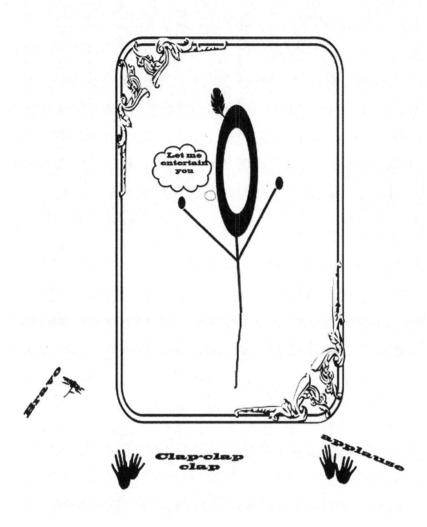

Stand up comedy
Done, got my pluck on, what's next?
A one woman show

Ani's Adventures Performing

'Applause, Applause'

After the success with stand up comedy (which was just showing up & doing it) what next? My birthday was coming up, the first one since the split with JB. I wanted to avoid the pain of that ... what to do to celebrate myself? I decided to do a one woman show called ... you guessed it, 'Ani's Adventures in Autonomy'. I wrote some skits about breaking up & the dating game experiences (this was before computer dating) re: the Village Voice Personals. I must say I did have some hilarious encounters. My friend Arthur & assistant at work was my music man which consisted of pressing the button on the tape recorder ... not a good choice. When it was time for the first number, 'You Gotta Have A Gimmick' I gave him the signal ... moments passed, no music. I began some sassy repartee ... endless time passed ... I wondered what was wrong ... finally the sweet sound of the tape began. Whew!

This little Tribeca off, off broadway theater was filled to capacity with my friends who had come out to support me.

I was feeling the love. So I guess I had accomplished what I had set out to do express my creativity & avoid the pain. Another crisis averted but it was only a matter of time before it would catch up with me. There's no way around it, only one way-thru it, feel it & let it go. I was learning this lesson slowly but surely. I had held it at bay as long as possible but now the time had come. I surrendered to the pain, it flowed thru me & out easier than all the energy it took to resist it. A lesson well learned that would help me many more times in the future.

High hopes second time
Started well, broke down quickly
There are no mistakes

X.

Unfolding of a Relationship

'So Happy Together'

Finally the day came: my graduation, my MA in Theater Arts. I proudly went to the ceremony @ CCNY and had lunch with friends afterwards. One of my biggest accomplishments so far in my new single life along w/ snagging a rent controlled apt in Manhattan. How lucky was I? Rhetorical ... LOL!

Since I had been studying and working hard the past 3 years, I decided a fun night out was in order. I went to an Outdoor Singles Meetup that very night as we were heading into summer & I was looking for some outdoor activity. And that's where I met JB, the main character in my life for the next 8 years (and I do mean character- in a good way). I was 48 & in my prime, he was 39 & raring to go. When one chapter ends, a new one begins. We met, spoke briefly, exchanged numbers; next day I got a message, it was a pleasure to meet you.

Hmm! About a week later my dear friend Ed called & offered me 2 tix to a bway show he was unable to attend. I gleefully accepted. Called up a girlfriend to join me but she was busy. I know, I'll call the new guy, which I proceeded to do. He was delighted to get my invitation and came downtown from the Bronx pronto. We enjoyed the evening together and made plans for our first official date the following weekend: dinner & a movie in Chinatown-how exotic was that? I loved it! After the second get together, he asked if he could crash on the couch as it was late, trains were slow etc. I agreed. It wasn't long before the couch turned into my bed, it was mutual & inevitable. And the rest is history as they say.

The relationship took off like a rocket, fast and furious. We were an item. Getting to know each other was fun; we both loved nature, the outdoors, culture, the arts, spirituality and travel. Next step getting to know each others friends & families. I adored his warm Italian family & they me-it was great to be a part of it. I had a graduation party to celebrate my MA degree and that was a golden opportunity for him to meet my teacher friends. Sunday dinner in the Bronx was my invitation into the family. How sweet it was, I bless them still. We took a vacation to Ma. that summer & visited my mom and explored the area where he used to live. By the time summer was over, we were ready to move in together. Tribeca or the Bronx?-no contest. I was very excited as we fixed up the place, our love nest. I was so happy to have a second chance on love... I ignored the red flags. Oh yes there were issues...anger, trust and chemical dependency. Did I learn nothing from the first go round? We had many break ups & reconciliations over those 8 years but my codependence had a strong grip on me & I so wanted it to work out. Love conquers everything & all that.

I must say many of my needs were met: travel, we took many great vacations: Fl., Va., Maine-Bar Harbor, Hawaii-Oahu, Niagara Falls. We drove cross country, a dream come true. And everyday was a holiday w/ JB. We took the ferry to Gov.'s Island to grocery shop as he had those benefits being a purple heart hero in

Vietnam. We also went to the pool there & had picnics to escape the sweltering summer heat of NYC ... our own private club. But when he was bad, he was horrid. Temper tantrums are not so attractive in a grown man. On the other hand he was a great cook & enjoyed the social things that I did. I guess I could put up w/ his tantrums ... until I couldn't. I was in a quandry, what to do? I was so unhappy now. I was asking myself these questions while riding my bike to teach @ NYU when I fell in a pot hole & broke my hip. Suddenly the picture changed, he rose to the occasion & took such good care of me, a born nurturer he. Things were going well during this period, I got all the attention, affection & care I ever wanted. So sweet. But once I got back into commission it was the same old, same old. It was SO old! I decided to leave NYC alone & move to Va. Bch. We had planned on moving together but this was not meant to be. I asked him to move out ... not a day at the beach. Finally it happened & I grieved more than when my marriage had ended. Go figure. Grief is grief. In retrospect we offered each other just what we needed at that point in our lives ... along w/ the baggage. 'Je ne rien regrette; After that we had a few visits, he moved to the mtns in Va., which started out well but always deteriorated in the same way. It was over. Put a period. Next Chapter.

Part II.

Back to the seashore
The sand the forest and the trees
Ain't nature grand

I.

Next Stop Va. Bch...Psychic or Psycho?

'I Can See Clearly Now'

Virginia Beach was calling to me between a major health challenge and a failed relationship - give me the simple life. And anything out of NYC was simpler than that complex burg. Don't get me wrong, I adore the Big Apple but at this particular time in my life I needed peace and quiet and nature which I felt Va. Bch offered and I'm a beach babe from way back, I met my first love at the beach. So, it's very meaningful to me. Due to a hip injury, I took an early retirement from teaching and off to Va. Bch I went. What's next I asked myself? I had a strong interest in psychic development and self healing the hip situation. I was determined to heal myself and in the process develop psychic abilities. The ARE/Edgar Cayce Inst. was just the place. One unconventional method I explored was humor. This interested me greatly and I read everything I could get my hands on. I wound up giving talks at the

ARE on the Healing Power of Humor. I also attended every workshop given on psychic development, this fascinated me & was fun too. While studying and working at the ARE, I had the opportunity to perform in a play, 'Godspell' which the Inst. put on. This was right up my alley and gave me great joy to participate. The fellowship felt reminded me of my summer stock days and the family bonding that took place. Yes, my needs were being met and I found my new tribe at the ARE.

WooWoo mystical
Occult metaphysical
What is in a name?

II.

Edgar Cayce, the Heritage Psychic Line...and Abraham

'Do You Believe in Magic?'

Things are going along swimmingly at the Association for Research & Enlightenment and in the Chesapeake Bay. I had instituted a day each week for myself & 2 gal pals to get in the Bay. We called ourselves the 'Bay Babes'. Each of us loved the water as much as the other. We visited in the bay, exercised in the bay and basked in the sun. We reveled in those healing days and precious times together, Thru the ARE I became familiar with the Heritage Center. I learned that they offered a psychic phone line. I felt ready to go for it and test myself out. I made an appointment and met with the coordinator, Mary Burke. She had me do readings for 2 people and herself and before I knew it I was hired starting immediately. This worked out very well for me as I could work from home (my hip was starting to act up & the pain was increasing). I enjoyed helping all my clients at that time who became repeat customers and some friends as well. One of the other gifts I received from my ARE time was an introduction to ABRAHAM via Esther & Jerry Hicks. It was the most liberating, joyful philosophy I had come across so far. A group of us would meet weekly at a local home and listen to tapes of their workshops. It was enlivening, inspiring and expansive. From that core group I have retained a few friends to this day. It has opened me up to more joy than other teachings so far. Among my other shifts was an opportunity for this city gal to do some kayaking. Again love that water, in it or on it.

Woman heal thyself
Mind power or operation?
It's all good, all God

III.

Health Recovery

'Let's Get Physical'

Another benefit of the ARE was the massage school on the premises. My friends & I indulged ourselves in weekly massages- health maintenance. A weekly Yoga class was also offered; yoga was a lifelong love & practice of mine. All the conditions for good health were there ... except for one. My hip was getting worse. Try as I did for self healing, I had to admit it was not working. My doctor advised there would be a hip replacement in my future-no psychic he, the x-ray told him so. I came to terms with this news and started planning the best time to undergo my surgery. I consulted psychics & astrologers and came up with a date. My friends were standing by to support me. Unfortunately nature did not cooperate ... there was a storm... electric out ... surgery postponed. The best laid plans ... the next postponement - the doctor ordered a stress test before he'd operate so all that took extra time. When the day finally came I was, okay, let's do this ... and it came off without a hitch. I had all the conditions for a speedy recovery right at hand: massage, yoga & bike paths to ride in beautiful Seashore State Park. One of the ingredients that contributed to my recovery was I happened to be in a performance art group then called 'the Cat's Meow' and while I was recovering I would go to rehearsals and do what I could until I was ready to resume my part in full. I know this was a major factor in recovering my health. Do what you love and health will follow. I continue to count all the blessings I received during my time in Va. Bch; good friends, my health, my creative expression as a psychic, actress and singer and best of all my philosophy of joy & freedom from Abraham. Oh! and did I mention my 2 cats Sassy and Romeo, the loves of my life? Well-being abounds!

Reaching promised land
Inner and outer both ways
Thank God free at last

IV.

Reaching the Promised Land

'What A Wonderful World'

'Another Day in Paradise' you'll often hear residents of Florida, the Sunshine State say. But it's so much more than that, it's a state of mind. And that state of mind includes awakening to the beauty of nature, birds,animals, plants, flowers, trees and bushes. It's noticing the beautiful environment we live in, appreciating it and sharing it with each other. And when we notice the good stuff, it expands ... the unfolding of it expands. We are expansive beings and things are always getting more than before ... point it out, bask in it, celebrate it. This is what the Promised land is all about, heaven on earth. It is realizing that we are free, happy and greatly loved...we are exhilarated and light hearted. Not that stuff doesn't happen, it does ... but being light hearted about it relieves the stress. When living with this awareness, what's next is an exciting adventure. My own personal evaluation brought me to this place in time physically, spiritually and emotionally. It was well worth the trip, this awakening is living in bliss every day and sending out that positive energy to touch everyone who comes across your path on a daily basis. Instead of a daily word, I send out a daily flower to my FaceBook friends ... they are beautiful and endless in variety ... like life!

At the core of my life is my spiritual practice, Kriya Yoga Meditation. It gives me strength and sustains me. When I first visited my BFF Yvonne in Florida back in the 90's she invited me to a group of friends who practiced KYM. I took to it right away. So every time I visited Fl. this was a part of the visit. It just felt so good to make a space for group meditation in my life. When I moved to Fl. in 2001, the practice became more regular and I learned my friends had gone to an ashram in Homestead to get initiated. This was something to think about, a deeper commitment to my practice. Friend Rob and I were the newbies of the group and decided we were ready to make that commitment. A few friends in the group offered to drive down to Homestead with us to support our initiation. This was a four hour journey and the festivities started early in the morning. We left at 3am as I recall, excited and eager to begin. It was a surreal experience, day long. Due to the lack of sleep and mystical nature of the initiation Rob & I were exhausted by the afternoon and ready to go back to the hotel. As we started the car, the Swami came running over to us, 'You're not leaving, are you?' I said 'Yes' and Rob said 'No'. Busted. We shut off the motor and burst out laughing and went back to the next segment ... our tails between our legs. Who says humor isn't spiritual? Laughter is healing. In fact we reminisce and laugh about that incident to this day. And yes, we still have our weekly KYM group and our spiritual family right here ... a blessing in all our lives.

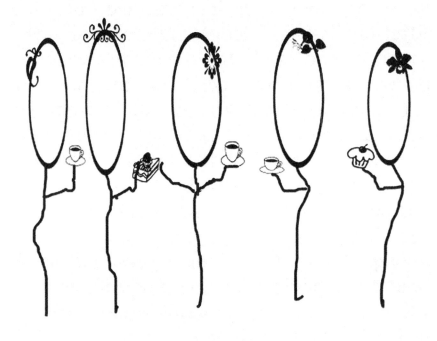

Powerful women
The Chi Chi's are amazing
Making miracles

V.

The Chi-Chi's

'Superwoman'

When I moved to Florida I was fortunate to have a BFF already living there. We had left NYC together in '94; me to Va. Bch. and she to Fl. We visited each other often over the next 8 years. When I tired of even 'mild winters' it was time to go south. In the meantime Yvonne had been creating a spiritual network and community of her own ... so when I arrived this paradigm was already in place. The Chi-Chi's was a group of six women who met once a month. The purpose was to catch up with each others' lives, see how our intentions were manifesting and set new ones if need be ... and have a pot luck. We supported and empowered each other through thick and thin and grew to such a level of trust that it was remarkakable. Those gals are my Chi-Chi Sistahs & BFF's, this was our mastermind group. Over the years we changed the meeting place from restaurants to each other's houses and currently we've been meeting at one member's home who just happens to live on Tampa Bay with a view of downtown St. Pete. This works out very well for all of us: beauty, elegance, luxury ... what's not to like? It meets our needs ;-) But the work we do is at the core of our get togethers. We have become such powerful manifestors together that we literally feel there is nothing we cannot do, be or have if we intend it with the support of the Chi-Chi's (chi means energy). Yes we are the Chi-Chi's: Superwomen! Another one of the many miracles in my life now.

Lucy & Ethyl once sang 'Friendship, just the perfect blendship When other friendships have been forgot ... ours will still be hot!'They are the perfect role models for friends, there for one another through thick and thin-fiascoes of one sort or another with style and humor.

Being an only child, I learned early how to make a friend and be a friend in order to meet my need for companionship. This was important to me and I gave it the importance in my life that it deserved. As a result I have been well blessed with many wonderful friends throughout my life ... and continuous friendships from as far back as first grade and high school. These relationships have given me love, caring, joy, support and nurturing...and relief when things got out of hand. The thread of continuity is amazing, 'we go back', 'we have a history' are not empty phrases nor is BFF -best friend forever. It is a committment and I hope it lasts forever as my BFF's know too much stuff about me now :-) I'd hate to think they weren't on my side LOL. And so that's what I love about my friendships: they love you - the good, the bad and the ugly ... and vice versa.

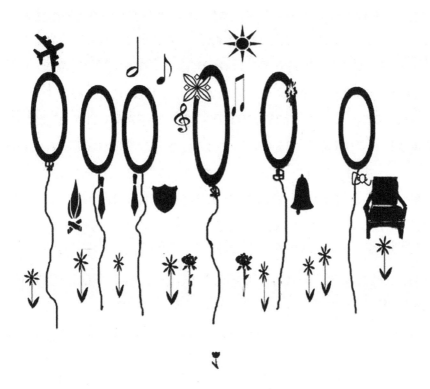

Happy days are here
Filled with joy, peace, ease and love
I have arrived NOW!

Epilogue

'Je Ne Rien Regrette'

Having lived in this state for a dozen years I can testify: dreams do come true and miracles abound. I always had a yen to be on the radio, a favored medium of mine. When I moved to Florida I decided I'll do this now. And so I went about my life with that intention and met someone who invited me to be a guest on his radio show which led to...my own radio show 'Ask the Blonde How to Live Fully & Well'. On my show I interviewed people who were living their dream and how they accomplished it. The show ran for 2 and a half years...till I was ready for my next adventure: Dance. I had expressed this wish to a friend and together we discovered 'Forever Moving', a dance group for folks forty plus. The weekly practice and rehersals were lessons in aliveness, a feeling I always want to enjoy- no matter what age. We had a performance at USF in Tampa which was the epitome of exhilaration for us dancers and the audience loved it too.

Next, having played the matchmaker in an

earlier chapter in my life (Fiddler on the Roof - summer stock, Plymouth, Ma.) I decided to become one ... and the MatchMakingMuse was created. One evening while watching the BBC news I caught a human interest piece: Matchmaking Festival in Ireland- Farmers come to town to find wives. I was quite taken by the concept and decided right on the spot-'I'm going to do that right here in Gulfport!'... and I did ...twice ... and on Valentines Day, of course. Aliveness energy soared through me as I prepared for these events. The event itself was enjoyed by the singles with no Valentine date, a chance to have a party & some fun & dance and possibly meet someone. It was heaven sent for all the people without partners.

My next endeavor was traveling to the interior ... DreamGirls was created by a few women who had the same desire. We Gals came together for the purpose of writing down our dreams, sharing them and doping them out together ... investigating the unconscious. We learned a great deal about ourselves in these monthly meetings and continue to do so as the group is ongoing.

Turned out to be a powerful tool for self reflection and awareness.

The inner quest led naturally to the outer quest of compassionate communication. I began studying non-violent communication. My B.A. is in Communication so it has been a lifelong interest of mine. This refinement of the process: sender, receiver, response has been so instrumental and beneficial in my communication with family, friends and colleagues as well with the objective of a win-win outcome realizing we all have a beautiful need that is motivating us. I was introduced to NVC from a fellow in another of my self help groups when I complained of my communication difficulties with my kids. He offered me this option and it was spot on. Before long an introductory workshop was offered in my area, I went & joined a processing group for the next 2 years, invaluable work. The NVC way is useful if it's between 2 people or 2 nations and has been used in conflict resolution around the world. When the student is ready the teacher appears.

Catching up with myself, I am currently the resident psychic at Shiva Dharma here in Gulfport. The energy from my ARE days and the Psychic phone line has re-surfaced and I am enjoying this time as the Psychic Queen of Fun. I love sitting in front of the shop and chatting with passers-by and watching the delightful doggie parade go by and giving some insightful information to the person who stops by for a reading.. The Shiva Dharma family is one of love and support. I'm truly blessed ... and I have attracted it all into my life...thank you very much ;-) 'Life is but a dream, it's what you make it'.

Singing & the movies...

My next adventure ... singing! Singing - everyone can sing and everyone should use their voice raised in song. Why? It's good for your health, vibration,breathing & good exercise. It is a gift to ourselves and others. Since I was a child I loved to sing & enjoyed songs & singing them, I knew every commercial. As an adult, I picked up this thread when I moved to Va. Bch. and joined the Joyful Noise Chorus. We sang broadway show tunes sprinkled with sacred music. It was a delightful experience; we sang at senior residences and at the stage at the oceanfront. It was such a high, words can hardly express it. Moving to Florida, I wanted to continue the fun. Ask for what you want...My new bud Rob also loved to sing and we heard about the local college having a chorus made up of students & open to the community. We were there on day one to sign up and for the next five years we sang our hearts out. Christmas holidays were were heightened and brightened by candlelight concerts,every spring was made more glorious by the spring concert.

That thread has continued as my grandson Danny is a singer, musician, composer... and the beat goes on.

I do miss it but moved on to sample some of the other goodies in life such as... the movies. I've had a life long love affair with film. Daddy took me to the movies every Sunday afternoon and the seed was sown, I was hooked. Love this medium, musicals are high on the list along with art films, foreign films and independent films. Once again the Universe supported my passion...Eckerd College offers an International Film Series course open to the community. I'm in heaven! This legacy has been passed on to my daughter Joanne who is also an avid film enthusiast. We have great conversations about the latest art films. She in turn introduced film to her boys and a nephew as well to carry on the tradition. And the legacy goes on. Another love Joanne and I share is books, we love to read and give tips and give books and discuss...also passed along to her boys, my grandsons. These joys are the legacy I have given my children and grandchildren. I now share book tips with grandson Bobby, who also writes. I have a knack for enjoying life. My philosophy is find out what it is you love to do and just do it. And the joy goes on, that is my legacy to my children and grandchildren.

'The Joie de Vivre'

Thank you for reading my story. I hope you got a few gems to take away with you and start the process of creating your own best life from this day forward!

Much Love and Many Blessings, Ani Crane, M.A.

Special Thanks

Special thanks to those who helped serve to make this book what it is: John Rehg, John Carroll, Gregory Smith, my beautiful friends who read the first chapter and encouraged me to go on, the Memoir Circle who listened and gave gentle feedback, Nuance Gallery who held Spoken Word Night and Michael Whelan who invited me to come & present Chapter I ... and finding my title there 'How I Arrived Here'.

And a word of thanks to the Arts Anonymous group especially Donna D. who supported me in this whole process.

Many Thanks All

Made in the USA
Columbia, SC
08 October 2022